PARTICIPANT'S GUIDE

THE LIFE
YOU'VE
ALWAYS
WANTED

Resources by John Ortberg

An Ordinary Day with Jesus
(curriculum with Ruth Haley Barton)

Everybody's Normal Till You Get to Know Them
(book, audio)

God Is Closer Than You Think
(book, audio, curriculum with Stephen and Amanda Sorenson)

If You Want to Walk on Water, You've Got to Get Out of the Boat
(book, audio, curriculum with Stephen and Amanda Sorenson)

The Life You've Always Wanted
(book, audio, curriculum with Stephen and Amanda Sorenson)

Living the God Life

Love Beyond Reason

Soul Keeping
(book, audio, curriculum with Christine M. Anderson)

When the Game Is Over, It All Goes Back in the Box
(book, audio, curriculum with Stephen and Amanda Sorenson)

THE LIFE YOU'VE ALWAYS WANTED

SPIRITUAL DISCIPLINES FOR ORDINARY PEOPLE

BESTSELLING AUTHOR

JOHN ORTBERG

with Stephen and Amanda Sorenson

ZONDERVAN

The Life You've Always Wanted Participant's Guide
Copyright © 2004 by John Ortberg

Requests for information should be addressed to:
Zondervan, 3900 *Sparks Dr. SE, Grand Rapids, Michigan 49546*

ISBN 978-0-310-81019-3

Interior design: Nancy Wilson

Printed in the United States of America

HB 08.29.2017

Contents

Preface

If you have ever been frustrated with the state of your spiritual life. If you've ever wondered why spiritual growth seems to go so slowly. If you've ever wondered if real change is possible. If you've ever felt confused or stuck in your spiritual life—you're my kind of person.

I have struggled (and still do struggle) with those same things. But I have also discovered that it is possible to live the life I've always wanted to live. You see, the Christian gospel insists that the transformation of the human personality really is possible. It is never easy. It is rarely quick. But it is possible. I see it happening in people sometimes—occasionally even in myself.

It happens any time people become intensely serious about learning from Jesus how to arrange their lives. It happens any time people set their focus on learning to live as Jesus would live if he were in their place.

Throughout the centuries, wise people have devoted themselves to following Jesus in this way. This series is an attempt to make some of that wisdom accessible to people who live in a world of freeways, corporate ladders, and X boxes. When you are through, my hope is that you will accept Christ's invitation to live life his way because it truly is the life you've always wanted.

—John Ortberg

It's "Morphing" Time

The good news as Jesus preached it is that now it is possible for ordinary men and women to live in the presence and under the power of God ... It is not about the minimal entrance requirements for getting into heaven when you die. It is about the glorious redemption of human life — your life. It's morphing time.

—John Ortberg

QUESTIONS TO THINK ABOUT

1. To be *transformed* means to be changed, and transformation is taking place all around us all the time. What examples of transformation—of any sort—come to mind?

2. What is required for transformations such as those you have mentioned to occur?

3. Although we use the term *spiritual transformation,* we often use it casually without giving it much thought. Describe what *spiritual transformation* means to you.

4. What do you consider to be the indicators of spiritual transformation? How can we tell if another person has experienced a spiritual transformation?

VIDEO OBSERVATIONS

Life: disappointment and hope

We shall "morph" indeed

Pseudo-transformation

Trying harder versus training wisely

VIDEO HIGHLIGHTS

1. What is the hope of the Christian gospel as John Ortberg describes it?

2. An important concept in *The Life You've Always Wanted* is that we are always being transformed; we are always changing for better or for worse. This happens physically and, although it's less obvious, spiritually. How might some of our daily practices cause us to be "formed" spiritually in one direction or another?

3. Why did Jesus so strongly challenge pseudo-transformation and the rabbis' "boundary markers" regarding dietary laws, the Sabbath, and circumcision?

4. In what ways does pseudo-transformation creep into churches today, and what are its damaging effects? Can you identify any "boundary markers" in your church?

LARGE GROUP EXPLORATION

Pseudo-Transformation vs. Morphing

When our lives are not marked by genuine, God-directed spiritual change, we tend to look for substitute ways to distinguish ourselves from those we consider to be less spiritual. We adopt boundary markers—highly visible, relatively superficial practices intended to quickly separate the "insiders" from the "outsiders." These boundary markers may include conformity to specified forms of dress and speech, adherence to certain rules of behavior, participation in prescribed activities, and so on. They provide a false sense of security and superiority.

The religious leaders of Jesus' day focused a great deal of their attention on boundary markers. Many of their conflicts with Jesus occurred because Jesus took a radically different approach to assessing spirituality. Instead of focusing on visible indicators of spiritual transformation, Jesus focused on what was happening in the heart. His concern was whether or not people were being transformed and growing in their love of God and love of people. His concern was whether or not they were "morphing" into the masterpieces God created them to be.

Let's consider these opposing perspectives on spiritual transformation.

1. Read Matthew 12:1–2; 15:1–2; Luke 18:11–12. Note the types of spiritual behaviors the religious leaders of Jesus' day considered important. What was Jesus' assessment of their spirituality? (See Mark 7:5–8.)

2. What did Jesus say that no doubt shocked the religious leaders? (Read Matthew 21:28–32.)

3. Instead of focusing on external religious practices, what did Jesus emphasize? (Read Luke 10:25–28; John 13:34–35.)

4. What is the evidence of true spiritual transformation in our lives? (Read 1 Corinthians 13:1–7.)

5. Now let's consider "morphing." The word *morph* comes from the Greek word *morphoo,* which means "the inward and real formation of the essential nature of a person." The term was used to describe the formation and growth of an embryo in a mother's body.

   The kind of spiritual transformation God wants each of us to experience is a complete "remaking" of our nature. He wants us to see, feel, think, and do what Jesus would if he were in our unique place. What makes such a transformation possible, and why is it important? (See Romans 6:3–14; 2 Corinthians 5:17–20; Ephesians 2:10.)

6. Another form of the word *morph* is used in the phrase "until Christ is formed in you" in Galatians 4:19. This word, *summorphizo,* means "to have the same form as another, to shape a thing into a durable likeness."

Our spiritual growth is to be a molding process, a process whereby we are shaped in the image of Christ. Notice what the following verses reveal about the process of spiritual growth God accomplishes within each Christian.

a. Galatians 4:19

b. Colossians 3:5–10

c. 2 Corinthians 3:18

7. In Romans 12:2, Paul used the word *metamorphoo,* from which we get the English word *metamorphosis.* The emphasis is that we don't simply learn to *do* things in a new way, we *become* the kind of people who *are* that way. How does this transformation come about?

The Impact of Pseudo-Transformation

We might be tempted to wonder if morphing makes any practical, daily-life differences as opposed to pseudo-transformation. Consider the perspective author Sheldon Vanauken offers in his critically acclaimed book *A Severe Mercy:* The strongest argument for Christianity is Christians, when they are drawing life from God. The strongest argument against Christianity? Also Christians, when they become exclusive, self-righteous, and complacent.

Consider, too, the warning signs of pseudo-transformation that appear in Matthew 23, where Jesus denounced the religious leaders of his day for their lack of true spiritual life. As you identify these warning signs, think about the ways these signs show up among Christians today.

Matthew 23	Warning Signs of Pseudo-Transformation
Verses 1–4	Demanding obedience from others, but not practicing what they preach; burdening other people with the pursuit of exhaustive, external rules and practices yet not helping to bear the burden.
Verses 5–8	Doing their spiritual duties so that other people will notice and honor them; expecting others to honor them; taking pride in their knowledge, position, and influence.
Verses 13–15	Making it difficult for other people to enter (and in some cases preventing people from entering) God's kingdom; refusing to enter the kingdom of heaven themselves.
Verse 23	Following the letter of the law but violating the spirit of the law such as by tithing every little thing to God, yet neglecting justice, mercy, and faithfulness.
Verses 24–29	Preoccupied with *appearing* to be spiritual; cleaning up the outside, but doing nothing to clean the mess on the inside; being hypocritical.

SMALL GROUP EXPLORATION

Training for Spiritual Growth

We all know that training is necessary if we want to succeed in physical competition. It is also true that training is necessary if we are serious about growing in our relationship with God. Learning to think, feel, and act like Jesus is at least as demanding as learning to run a marathon or play the piano. We can't succeed simply by trying hard. We can't succeed on willpower alone. We need to prepare ourselves to receive God's transforming work within us. We need to train wisely.

1. When the apostle Paul wrote about training to run a race (1 Corinthians 9:24–27), he and his readers knew exactly what he was talking about. Corinth was the site of the Isthmian Games, second only to the Olympics in prominence in ancient Greece. Paul probably visited Corinth during the games of AD 51 and may have made tents for the visitors and contestants. What is the spiritual "prize" for which Paul ran, and why did he take spiritual training so seriously? (See 1 Corinthians 9:25–27.)

2. What did Paul encourage his young protégé, Timothy, to do? Why? (See 1 Timothy 4:7–8.)

3. We may think that following Jesus and growing spiritually come about automatically and easily rather than through dedicated training, but that is not what Jesus taught. Read Mark 8:34–35 and Luke 14:27–30, 33. Notice what Jesus told the crowds that followed him about the path of spiritual growth.

4. We need to train ourselves for spiritual growth, but there's a big difference between fist-clenching, teeth-gritting exertion to become "more spiritual" and the transformed life Jesus offers. The following passages are essential to our understanding of how training for authentic spiritual transformation works.

   a. Read Matthew 11:28–30 and Romans 8:11. Notice how pursuing the life Jesus offers differs from the demands of pseudo-transformation.

   b. What do we learn about our ability to pursue spiritual growth from 2 Corinthians 12:9–10 and Philippians 4:13?

c. What encouragement does 2 Thessalonians 2:16–17 offer us?

5. To what did Jesus compare the possibility of living in the kingdom of God—of living the life you've always wanted? (See Matthew 13:44–46.)

GROUP DISCUSSION

1. Let's talk a bit more about spiritual disciplines. How does John Ortberg's definition of spiritual disciplines differ from how you have thought of them? In what ways does this definition change your behavior or how you approach and what you expect from your spiritual life?

What Is a Spiritual Discipline?

John Ortberg defines a spiritual discipline as any activity that can help us gain power to live life as Jesus taught and modeled it. Spiritual disciplines are a means of appropriating or growing toward the life God graciously offers. They allow us to do what we cannot do by will-power alone. So practices such as reading Scripture and praying are important not because they prove how spiritual we are but because God can use them to lead us into the kingdom life he offers.

---

2. Søren Kierkegaard once said, "Now, with God's help, I shall become myself." In what ways is this an accurate representation of authentic spiritual transformation?

3. Why do you think we are prone to substitute pseudo-transformation for authentic transformation? Why is it so easy to fall into the trap of saying or doing things we think spiritual people are supposed to say or do? Of hiding our sin? Of working hard to make people think we're loving instead of actually loving them?

PERSONAL JOURNEY: TO DO NOW

1. *We aren't who we want to be; our hope is to be transformed.* God created us to be his masterpieces, yet we fall short, loving God too little and sin too much. Caught between disappointment and hope, we long for the life he appointed us to live. Our hope is that our fallen state isn't all there is and that the transformation promised in the Christian gospel really is possible.

   In *The Life You've Always Wanted,* John Ortberg mentioned Popeye the Sailor Man, who said, "I yam what I yam." Popeye seemed sad, aware of his shortcomings and not anticipating much growth or change. Think about your disappointments honestly. In what way(s) have you struggled between disappointment and hope?

   We all face disappointment in ourselves, such as not being the parents we want to be or "loving sin too much and God too little." Which disappointments are most painful to you?

   Describe the spiritual hope to which you look forward.

2. *The primary goal of spiritual life is human transformation—real change in the essential nature of the person.* God is in the business of transforming ordinary people like us so that we express his character and goodness in our whole being. This is real transformation from the inside out—learning to think as Jesus would think, to feel what he'd feel, to perceive what he'd perceive, and therefore to do what he would do. It is a far cry from pseudo-transformation, the adherence to external rules or behaviors intended to identify us to others as "transformed" people.

If someone asked you, "How is your spiritual life going?" how would you respond? What would you say about yourself that would be impressive? What would you hesitate to reveal?

What standard do you use to evaluate your spiritual condition?

3. *If we are serious about spiritual transformation, we must not merely "try harder," we must "train wisely."* Growth in our relationship with God results from training in the spiritual disciplines. It happens whenever we become intensely serious about learning from Jesus how to arrange our lives. Spiritual disciplines are the practices we live by that enable us to do what we cannot do by will-

power alone. These practices help us grow in the ability to love God and people—the true indicators of spiritual well-being.

Would you say that you are *training* to become more like Christ, or *trying* to be more like Christ? Why?

John Ortberg emphasizes that we can't transform ourselves; God transforms us. How would you describe the difference between spiritual training and self-transformation? In what way(s) have you attempted self-transformation?

You will have the opportunity to further develop a personal spiritual training plan as this series progresses. For now, write down a few ideas of what spiritual training might involve for you.

PERSONAL JOURNEY:
TO DO ON YOUR OWN

Set aside some time to reflect on the following questions:

1. In *The Life You've Always Wanted,* John Ortberg wrote, "Your story is the story of transformation. You will not always be as you are now; the day is coming when you will be something incomparably better—or worse."

   In which direction are you presently being transformed?

   Is this where you want to go? Why or why not?

2. It is not always easy to know when we are settling for pseudo-transformation rather than real transformation, but the burden of trying to satisfy the demands of a superficial, boundary-marker oriented spirituality will exhaust us. The following questions can help you identify signs of an inauthentic spirituality. This self-assessment is for your eyes only. Be as honest as possible so you can clear the slate and open yourself up to God's transforming work in your life.

In what way(s) am I preoccupied with *appearing* to be spiritual?

In which area(s) am I becoming judgmental, exclusive, or proud?

To what degree am I becoming less approachable to other people?

In what way(s) am I becoming weary of pursuing spiritual growth?

In what way(s) do I measure my spiritual life by superficial standards?

Which "boundary markers" do I use to set myself apart from other people?

Now pray that God will guide you as you think about your life today and the life you've always wanted. Ask him to speak to your heart and begin transforming you through the remaining sessions of this study.

Slowing Down and Celebrating

As much as we complain about it, we are drawn to hurry. It makes us feel important. It keeps the adrenaline pumping. It means we don't have to look too closely at the heart or life.

—John Ortberg

QUESTIONS TO THINK ABOUT

1. How many times a day do you estimate you think to yourself, *Oh, I'd better hurry and ...—*? What are some of the reasons you feel you have to "hurry" through life?

2. If someone were to say, "I think you would benefit from a day of solitude," how would you respond? What do you think such a day would be like?

3. What is the most joyful event you have ever witnessed or in which you have ever participated? What made it meaningful to you?

VIDEO OBSERVATIONS

"Hurry sickness"

The discipline of slowing

"Dee dah day" moments

The connection between God and joy

VIDEO HIGHLIGHTS

1. Why is "hurry sickness" so harmful to our spiritual growth?

Oh for the Joy of It!

Early in the Israelites' history, God (speaking through Moses) established times of celebration. During these times, God's people would do things that filled them with joy, and they would identify those things as blessings from God. Some of the feasts included:

The Feast of Weeks celebrating the dedication of the firstfruits of the wheat harvest, the last crop to ripen (Leviticus 23:15–21).

The Feast of Passover that combined Passover, which celebrated the angel of death passing over the Hebrew households in Egypt (Leviticus 23:5), and the Feast of Unleavened Bread, which commemorated the first seven days of the Exodus (Leviticus 23:6–8).

The Feast of Tabernacles, which commemorated the Israelites' wandering in the desert (Leviticus 23:33–36).

Here's a thought to ponder: How might Christians today live differently if we designated certain days to specifically celebrate God's goodness — to celebrate a bountiful harvest, to celebrate employment, to celebrate the unique beauty of where we live, to truly celebrate redemption as a gift from God?

---

2. Many of us tend to avoid solitude. Which characteristics of solitude offend us? Which of our attitudes cause us to resist solitude?

3. What did you think when John Ortberg spoke of God as being deeply joyful? Why do you think God commands, rather than suggests, that we be joyful?

4. In the Old Testament, God commanded the Israelites to celebrate on many occasions. From a spiritual perspective, what is the point of celebration?

SMALL GROUP EXPLORATION

Confronting Our Hurry Sickness

It's no secret that most of us lead hurried, harried lives. John Ortberg describes the American lifestyle as being so rushed and preoccupied that we don't actually live life, we just skim over it! Yet racing through life at breakneck speed isn't healthy physically or spiritually.

Hurry sickness is more than a disordered schedule; it reflects a disordered heart. Hurry disrupts our life-giving connection with God, so if we want to grow spiritually we must train ourselves to eliminate hurry. We have no greater example of this than the life of Jesus. Let's see how Jesus faced his busy life and consider what we can change to eliminate hurry in our lives.

1. Read Mark 6:30–46, which is an account of a day in the life of Jesus.

   a. What kind of day did Jesus have?

   b. How do you think you might have handled that day if you had been in Jesus' shoes?

c. What is significant about what Jesus did at the end of this busy day? (See Luke 5:15–16 also.)

2. Two friends of Jesus (the sisters Mary and Martha) shed some light on the impact of hurry sickness on our lives. Read Luke 10:38–42 and note what is happening spiritually and relationally. Note also how Jesus viewed this situation.

3. When John Ortberg says we must "ruthlessly eliminate hurry," he doesn't mean we just cross things off our to-do list. We eliminate hurry by setting the priorities of our heart in order. The Bible frequently cautions us against being consumed (or disordered) by the priorities of this world—accumulation of wealth, concern about food and shelter, desire for recognition or power—all of which drive us to be hurried people. The following Scripture passages provide perspective and instruction on how to "order" our hearts. What do they reveal is beneficial or harmful to us?

a. Matthew 16:26

    b. 1 Timothy 6:6–7

    c. Philippians 3:18–21

4. If we don't want hurry to rule our lives, we need to take steps to slow down. John Ortberg calls these steps the discipline of slowing down and the practice of solitude.

    a. When we feel hurried, when we are pressured and pressed from every angle, what does the Bible tell us to do? What is the result? (See 1 Peter 5:7 and Philippians 4:6, respectively.)

    b. In addition to quieting our spirit by giving our cares to God and trusting him to enable us to accomplish all we need to get done, we can deliberately choose ways not to hurry. We can, for example, place ourselves in positions where we have to wait or do things more slowly, such as driving in the slow lane. What is a good way for you to practice deliberate slowing?

c. Every day, responsibilities pull us in many directions, so we each need times of solitude—times to withdraw, take a deep breath, focus on God, recharge, and evaluate. When can you find (or carve out) a daily moment for solitude? Identify at least two possibilities for regular, longer times of solitude.

LARGE GROUP EXPLORATION

God Wants Us to Mirror His Joy

G. K. Chesterton wrote about children having such "abounding vitality" that they want to do, see, or hear the same things again and again and again. Although the monotony of repetition nearly kills grown-ups, it thrills children. And Chesterton thinks it is possible that, like a child, God exults in monotony. He writes in *Orthodoxy:*

> It is possible that God says every morning, "Do it again" to the sun; and every evening, "Do it again" to the moon. It may not be automatic necessity that makes all daisies alike; it may be that God makes every daisy separately, but has never got tired of making them. It may be that He has the eternal appetite of infancy; *for we have sinned and grown old, and our Father is younger than we.*

In other words, many of us live as the joy-impaired children of a joy-infused God! So let's see what God has to say about joy and how he wants it to influence our lives.

1. In Genesis 1, we read a day-by-day account of God's creation of the universe.

   a. What pattern is repeated throughout the process of creation, and what does it reveal about God? (See Genesis 1:3–5, 9–12, 14–18, 20–21, 24–25, 31.)

b. What other indications of God's pleasure and joy do we see in Genesis 1? (Note especially verses 22, 27–28.)

2. In *The Life You've Always Wanted*, John Ortberg describes Jesus as the "Joy-bringer." What did Jesus bring, and what does it have to do with joy? (See Matthew 4:23; 1 Peter 1:8–9.)

3. Toward the end of his life on earth, Jesus prepared himself and his followers for his departure. What was his specific desire and concern for his followers? (See John 15:9–11; 17:1, 13.)

4. When are we to express joy and why is it so important? (See Philippians 4:4; 1 Thessalonians 5:16–18.)

5. When the exiles returned to Israel, they focused on obeying God's law. As they began to understand God's law, they grieved over their sinfulness, but God commanded them to celebrate what he had done. What did the people do, and what was the result? (See Nehemiah 8:9–12, 17.)

6. What can God's people look forward to in eternity? (See Isaiah 35:9–10.)

GROUP DISCUSSION

1. What is the real difference between being *busy* and being *hurried?*

2. What did you learn about joy today? In what ways might understanding more about the joy of the Lord affect your view of joy?

3. As you look at daily life, can you identify any "dee dah day" moments you've been overlooking, or that many of us overlook? How might life change if we left room in our hearts to enjoy these "dee dah day" moments?

4. In light of what we have studied during this session, which aspects of spiritual life do you think ought to prompt a "dee dah day" response? How often do you respond to these with joy? How often do you see others respond to these with joy? Why do you think we sometimes lack joy?

PERSONAL JOURNEY: TO DO NOW

1. *We are a people plagued by "hurry sickness," and hurry causes great harm to our spiritual growth.* Hurry is not merely a shortage of time; it is a disease of the soul. It is not just a disordered schedule; it reflects a disordered heart. Hurry lies behind much of the anger and frustration of modern life. It disrupts our life-giving connection with God and prevents us from receiving love from the Father or giving it to his children. If we want to grow spiritually, we must ruthlessly eliminate hurry from our lives.

   In what ways has hurry sickness hurt you, people around you, and your relationship with God?

2. *The discipline of slowing and the practice of solitude are antidotes to hurry sickness.* To eliminate hurry from our lives doesn't mean we won't be busy. Jesus was often busy, but he was never hurried. His priorities were always ordered according to his life-giving connection with his Father. By practicing the discipline of slowing, we too can learn to become unhurried people. When we practice solitude, we remove ourselves from the forces of daily life that otherwise mold us. We withdraw from noise, people, activities, and responsibilities in order to restore our connection with God.

   Consider how different your life would be if you approached it from an unhurried perspective, if you ordered your priorities according to your relationship with God. Write down specific things you can think or do to eliminate hurry.

Symptoms of hurry sickness	Our perspective when we are hurried	My "unhurried" alternative
Constantly speeding up daily activities	There aren't enough hours in the day so we try to do things faster and become impatient when we have to wait.	
Multi-tasking	We do or think about more than one thing at a time, packing as much into our day as possible.	
Clutter	Things aren't simple. Stuff accumulates. We get weighed down by things we failed to refuse to do.	
Clutter	We trade wisdom for information and exchange depth for breadth.	
Sunset fatigue	By day's end, we are too tired, drained, or preoccupied to receive love from the Father or give it to people around us.	

3. *As creatures made in the image of God, we are to reflect God's joy in life.* Joy is at the heart of God's plan for us because joy is at the heart of God. We cannot truly know God until we understand that he is the happiest being in the universe. He longs for us to be filled with his joy. It is so important to him that he commands us to be joyful and urges us to participate in celebration, which trains us to experience joy in life.

Would people close to you describe you as a joyful person? If not, how would they describe you? In what ways would you like their perception to change?

Think over the last day and week and write down "dee dah day" moments that occurred around you.

What was your response to those moments?

What did you benefit from or miss out on related to those moments?

PERSONAL JOURNEY:
TO DO ON YOUR OWN

Knowledge is not what makes us unhurried or joyful people. We have to train—practice being who we want to become. Set aside some time to practice the disciplines of slowing down and celebration.

The Practice of Daily Solitude: Reviewing the Day with God

It can be difficult to carve out times of extended solitude, but every day you can practice solitude a few minutes at a time. Here's how:

1. Be still for a moment and quiet your mind.
2. Acknowledge that Jesus is present. Invite him to teach you.
3. Go back in your mind to when you first woke up and watch that scene, as if on video. This may lead you to pray for patience, greater love, courage, forgiveness, or other virtues.
4. Continue to reflect on the day, going from scene to scene. Some scenes may fill you with gratitude, others with regret. Speak to God about this. You might pray for people with whom you interacted.
5. End with a prayer of thanksgiving for God's mercy and love. Ask him to refresh you as you sleep.

Guidelines for Pursuing Joy

Joy is not the result of changed circumstances, but of a heart that pursues joy. There is no formula for pursuing joy, but the following activities will help make the joy of the Lord more evident in your life. Consider each of these practices and write down your personal disciplines of joy.

Disciplines of joy	Suggested activities	My joy disciplines
Practice the discipline of celebration.	Do activities that bring you pleasure — being with people you love, enjoying good food, etc., and reflecting on the God who has given you such wonderful gifts.	
Start pursuing joy *today*.	Psalm 118:24 tells us to rejoice and be glad in *this* day. If we wait until conditions are perfect, we won't rejoice at all.	
Find a "joy" mentor.	Intentionally spend time with life-enhancing, "joy-carrying," "joy-producing" people. Prize them. Thank them.	
Pray for joy.	Pray that the Holy Spirit will produce the fruit of joy in your life in greater abundance.	
Set aside one day a week to celebrate.	Eat foods you love, listen to music, surround yourself with beauty, etc. As you do these things, savor every moment and thank God for his wonderful goodness.	
Unplug the television for a week.	Instead of seeking "rest" in front of the television, nurture conversation with family and/or friends, think new thoughts, sleep more, read more, etc.	
Discipline your mind to view life from a biblical perspective.	To some degree, joy flows from a certain kind of thinking. How much more joy might you have if you viewed all events in light of Jesus' resurrection and his ultimate triumph?	

Planning a Time of Extended Solitude

In *The Life You've Always Wanted,* John Ortberg shared a plan for eight hours of solitude. Remember that this practice may not be easy for you. You may feel as if you are wasting your time because you are not *doing* something. Or you may feel intimidated, which is why the following structure may help you.

1. Find a place where you can be uninterrupted and alone, such as a park or retreat center.

2. Spend time the night before to prepare, to ask God to bless the day and to tell him that you want to devote the day to him. This day will be your gift to God, but even more, it is a gift God wants to give you. What do you need from him? A sense of healing and forgiveness? Conviction for an apathetic heart? Compassion? A renewed sense of mission? Ask God for this.

3. Arrange the day around listening to God. The following format is adapted from Glandion Carney's book *The Spiritual Formation Toolkit.*

8:00 – 9:00	Prepare your mind and heart, take a walk, or do whatever will help you set aside concerns over tasks and responsibilities. Try to arrange your morning so you can remain in silence from the time you awaken.
9:00 – 11:00	Read and meditate on Scripture, taking time to stop to reflect when God seems to be speaking to you through the text.
11:00 – 12:00	Write down responses to what you have read. Speak to God about them.
12:00 – 1:00	Eat lunch and take a walk, reflecting on the morning.
1:00 – 2:00	Take a nap.
2:00 – 3:00	Set goals that emerge from the day's reflection.
3:00 – 4:00	Write down three goals and other thoughts in a journal. You may want to do this in the form of a letter to God. Prepare to reenter society.

Praying and Confessing

Prayer, perhaps more than any other activity, is the concrete expression of the fact that we are invited into a relationship with God. . . . Confession is not primarily something God has us do because he needs it. . . . It is a practice that, done wisely, will help us become transformed.

—John Ortberg

QUESTIONS TO THINK ABOUT

1. What is your first response when you hear someone speak of the *discipline* of prayer?

2. What are some of the reasons people pray?

3. Describe times in your life when sin (and it doesn't have to be your sin) has affected your relationship with another person or with God.

4. When you hear the phrase "confess your sins to God," what comes to mind? Why?

VIDEO OBSERVATIONS

Prayer really does matter

No heroics—start where you are

Pray about what really matters

Stains on the sofa

The real value of confession

VIDEO HIGHLIGHTS

1. What is your response to the idea of praying five minutes a day, in the same place and at about the same time? In what ways would it be an effective (or ineffective) way to start building a time of regular prayer?

2. What has been your experience with the "monkeys jumping in the banana trees" when it comes to prayer? Why is it important to take time to settle down the "monkeys," and why is it important to pay attention if one "monkey" refuses to settle down?

3. Why do we have to confess our sins to God?

LARGE GROUP EXPLORATION

The Power of Prayer

Usually we think of events on earth being interrupted because of actions in heaven. But our prayers are so important, so powerful, that all of heaven listens to our prayers—and God responds. Prayer is about more than changing the course of history, however. Prayer is about our relationship with God. Perhaps more than any other activity, prayer expresses the fact that God has invited us into a personal relationship with him. Through prayer our human hearts are knit together with the heart of God. So let's explore some of what the Bible says about prayer and its impact.

1. Genesis 18:20–33 presents a most interesting prayer dialogue between God and Abraham. What difference did Abraham's persistent requests make?

2. What do Psalm 34:15 and James 5:17–18 reveal about the effectiveness of prayer?

3. Some people believe that if we really love God, powerful prayers will flow out of us without effort or discipline. What do Psalm 105:4, Colossians 4:2, and 1 Thessalonians 5:17–18 reveal that contradict this viewpoint?

4. How do we know God really wants us to ask him for help when we're in trouble? (See Psalm 10:17; Luke 18:7–8; Philippians 4:6.)

5. How honest do you think we can afford to be in our prayers to God? (See Numbers 11:10–15.)

6. Many prayers of intercession are recorded in the Bible. Let's look at three examples of intercessory prayers and note what makes them powerful and effective.

Prayer	What makes it powerful and effective?
Nehemiah 1:4–11	
2 Samuel 5:17–25	
Colossians 1:9–12	

SMALL GROUP EXPLORATION

Confession: Life Beyond Regret

Although we may not talk much about sin, all of us have sinned. Or, as John Ortberg pointed out in the video, we have all stained the sofa. The Bible clearly states that God freely forgives our sins, but many of us struggle to live in the reality of that forgiveness. That's why the practice of confession is necessary to our spiritual growth. Confession is not something God has us do because *he* needs it. Rather, confession is a practice that, done wisely, will help us become the transformed people we long to be. Let's explore what the Bible says about our sin and need for confession.

1. Where did our "stain of sin" originate and what can be done about it? (See Romans 3:22–24; 5:12.)

2. In story after story, the Bible exposes the consequences of having a sinful nature. Look up the following passages and write down the consequence of sin revealed in each.

Scripture	Consequence of a sinful nature
Proverbs 5:22–23	
Jeremiah 5:25	
John 8:34	
Romans 6:23	
Romans 8:7–8	
Galatians 5:19–21	
James 1:13–15	

3. One of the hazards of sin is that it distorts our ability to detect its presence.

   a. In what way(s) is this evident in the story of David and Bathsheba? (See 2 Samuel 11:1–9, 14–17; 12:1–7, 13.)

   b. What did Jesus warn us about in Matthew 7:3–5? How does this teaching relate to David's situation? How does it relate to us?

Did You Know?

God uses many ways to convict us of our sin: dreams and words (Job 33:14–18), consequences (Luke 15:11–18; Psalm 107:10–12, 17–20), the gospel message (Acts 2:36–37), our consciences and guilt (John 8:3–9), the Holy Spirit (John 16:7–9), and his discipline (Hebrews 12:5–6).

---

4. Knowing the full depth of our sinfulness, how does God respond to those who confess their sins to him? (See Isaiah 43:25; Joel 2:12–13; 1 John 1:7–9.)

5. What type of freedom do we experience when we confess our sins to God and turn away from them? (See Psalm 32:1–2; Acts 3:19; 2 Corinthians 7:10.)

6. What is it about confession, repentance, and forgiveness that enables us to face life with hope? (See Psalm 84:11–12; Romans 6:11–14.)

GROUP DISCUSSION

1. Based on this session, in what ways has your view of prayer changed? What have you learned that will help you practice a more disciplined prayer life? Which obstacles to prayer have you learned to overcome? What new hope do you have for your prayer life?

2. What impact does sin have on our lives — spiritually, emotionally, relationally — when we don't confess our sins to God? In what ways does sin harm our potential for spiritual growth?

3. Why is confession of our sins to God such an essential discipline? How have your views of confession changed as a result of what we've explored today?

4. John Ortberg encourages us to each find someone with whom we can talk about the "stains we have put on the sofa," someone with whom we can share everything, even our gravest sins. What experience have you had with doing this? What encourages you to do this? What holds you back?

PERSONAL JOURNEY: TO DO NOW

1. *Prayer is powerful, and when we pray all of heaven stops to listen.* God commands his people to pray. Prayer changes God's actions. Prayer knits our hearts with God's heart. Simple prayer is talking honestly to God about what is happening in our lives—about who we are and what is important to us, not about who we ought to be or what ought to concern us. Intercessory prayer is persistently approaching God about the needs of others.

   How pleased are you with your prayer life?

   In terms of your heart relationship with God?

   In terms of what you talk with him about?

   In terms of how you pray for others?

   In terms of what your prayers accomplish?

Describe what you would like to see your prayer life become.

2. *Prayer doesn't flow out of us without effort or discipline.* The practice of biblical prayer is learned behavior. Even Jesus' disciples, who had been taught about prayer since their earliest days, saw something different in the way Jesus prayed and asked him to teach them how to pray.

What changes would you like to make in your prayer life, starting today?

Which step(s) presented in this session can you take to begin building a more disciplined prayer time? For example, if you are not already doing so, are you willing to pray five minutes every day?

3. *The practice of confession opens the door to God's liberating forgiveness. It not only wipes away our guilt but enables us to become the transformed people we long to be.* Confession, a spiritual discipline that goes hand in hand with prayer, is absolutely essential if our hearts are to be knit together with the heart of God. Confession enables us to take appropriate responsibility for what we have done and to begin healing relationships that have been damaged by sin.

Is the discipline of confessing your sins to God a regular part of your life? Why or why not?

What changes might you want to make in this area?

In what way(s) might unconfessed sin be affecting your life and the lives of people around you?

PERSONAL JOURNEY: TO DO ON YOUR OWN

Establish a Prayer Pattern That Works for You

Read through the following tips for starting a regular prayer time. When you have finished, develop a prayer plan that works for you and begin to follow it. Make revisions as needed.

Tips on Starting a Regular Prayer Time

- *Keep your prayer time short.* Many people feel guilty about not praying and resolve to change their prayer habits. So they try to pray for far longer stretches of time than they are capable of doing. When they can't sustain long prayers, they give up until they feel guilty again. To avoid this cycle, keep your prayer time to five minutes every day at the same time, then pray more as you desire to do so.

- *Make your prayer time meaningful.* If beauty is important to you, pray outside or near a window with a view. Or light a candle to remind you that the light of God's presence and wisdom is available to guide you. Or pull up another chair to remind yourself that Jesus really is present with you. Use physical symbols such as these to support your practice of prayer.

- *Prepare ahead for your prayer time.* Before you pray, set aside a few minutes to settle your thoughts. You might take a few deep breaths and allow your mind to slow down. You might focus your eyes on a physical object or whisper "Heavenly Father" a few times until your mind quiets.

- *Pray about what is on your heart, not what you wish was on your heart.* Come before God as you are, opening your heart and making your requests to him. Avoid praying about the "right things" that you don't especially care about.

- *Learn to be fully present when you pray.* It's easy for our minds to wander when we pray. If your mind keeps returning to a particular thought, event, or person during prayer, it may indicate that you need to talk with God about the matter. During your prayer times, speak with God about what really concerns you.

My Personal Prayer Plan

What time of day is the best for me to set aside exclusively for prayer?

Where is the best place for me to pray at that time?

What is necessary for me to do to prepare my heart for prayer?

What will help me maintain my focus during my prayer time?

How will I decide what to pray about? (For example, you could make a list, or pray for what is most important to you at the time, etc.)

A Six-Step Process for Spiritual Stain Removal

Carefully review the process of confession below, which John Ortberg shares in *The Life You've Always Wanted*. As you read, think of how you can apply these steps in your life and the positive difference they will make. Then begin applying them soon.

Preparation	We place ourselves under the care and guidance of the Holy Spirit. Without God's help, we either tend toward self-condemnation for things we ought not to feel guilty about or gloss over ugly stains that need attention.
Self-examination	We reflect on our thoughts, words, and deeds. We examine our hearts in light of sin, such as the seven deadly sins (pride, anger, lust, envy, greed, sloth, and gluttony), or in light of the teachings of other Scripture, perhaps the Ten Commandments (Exodus 20) or the Beatitudes (Matthew 5). We honestly (and fearlessly) ask ourselves where we stand in regard to each of these. Then we take appropriate responsibility for our sinful choices and actions.
Perception	All sin involves denial and distorts our ability to detect its presence. So we need to see our sins through the eyes of God and through the eyes of anyone we have sinned against.
Ask *why?* And *what happened?*	Sin is often an attempt to meet a legitimate need in an illegitimate way. If we don't address that need appropriately, we'll keep sinning. So we need to ask ourselves why we pursued the course we took. We also need to face what happened as a result of our

	sin. True confession involves entering into the pain of anyone we've hurt and entering into God's pain over sin. Facing the consequences of our sin helps us develop a contrite heart that truly desires not to sin in that way again.
Make a new promise	Confession is not just naming sins we have done in the past. It involves our intentions about the future — a kind of promise. It involves a deep desire not to do these hurtful things again and an attempt to set right what we did wrong. It involves a resolution that, with God's help, we will change.
Healing grace	Grace is the final step in confession. God's grace allows the burden of our sin to cause pain and hardship in our lives. But as God's work is done in our hearts, God's grace also will completely release us from these burdens.

Meditating on Scripture and Seeking Guidance

God's purpose in guidance is not to get us to perform the right actions. His purpose is to help us become the right kind of people.

—John Ortberg

QUESTIONS TO THINK ABOUT

1. What is your response when a person says God told him or her to do something? Do you believe the Holy Spirit leads, guides, or directs ordinary people today? Explain your answer.

2. Describe a time in your life when you felt that God was communicating something to you. How did you know it was God?

3. What is the difference between meditating on Scripture and reading the Bible in order to gain more knowledge?

4. What does God really want his followers to do?

VIDEO OBSERVATIONS

Obstacles to transformation

Passivity

Double-mindedness

Washing our minds with Scripture

The work of seeking guidance

VIDEO HIGHLIGHTS

1. Now that we have a vivid image of double-mindedness in focus, what is double-mindedness? What is its source? And what impact does it have on our spiritual growth?

2. If we can't "override" double-mindedness by willpower or by trying to do better, how can our tendency toward double-mindedness be changed?

3. In what way is passivity an obstacle to guidance and spiritual growth?

4. John Ortberg said that God guides us in ways that are consistent with Scripture and consistent with the person he has created each of us to be. Why is it important for us to remember these principles?

LARGE GROUP EXPLORATION

Double-Mindedness: Enemy of the One Important Thing

In *The Life You've Always Wanted,* John Ortberg wrote about the importance of pursuing "one thing" in life. When we pursue one thing, we have a singleness of purpose, a clarity of commitment, and a consistency in our choices. Jesus calls his followers to pursue one thing in life—to seek his kingdom and his righteousness above all else. That one thing ought to dominate our thoughts, choices, and deeds.

But most of us have divided loyalties. We live one moment in the pursuit of God's kingdom and the next moment in the pursuit of our own desires. We want to do one thing, but do or say the opposite. To put it simply, we are double-minded. And double-mindedness prevents us from living the life we want to live. So let's see how we can eliminate double-mindedness from our lives.

1. What is the one important thing Jesus commanded his followers to do? (See Matthew 6:33.)

2. What cautions and principles do we find in Scripture concerning our allegiance to and focus on the things of this world versus the things of God? (See Matthew 4:8–10; 6:24; Colossians 3:2; Titus 2:11–14.)

3. What do James 1:5–8 and 4:7–8 reveal about double-mindedness as an obstacle to seeking God's guidance and experiencing spiritual growth?

4. The apostle Paul gives a great explanation of the nature of spiritual double-mindedness in Romans 7:18–24. What does he seem to think is the cause of double-mindedness, and what does he think he can do about it?

5. Some people think the battle of double-mindedness versus single-mindedness is a result of external influences. Where does Jesus tell us this battle originates? (See Matthew 15:18–20.)

6. We can't cure ourselves of double-mindedness. We need the "strong medicine" of Scripture to cleanse and purify our hearts. Read each of the following Scripture passages and write down the remedy for eliminating double-mindedness.

Scripture	Remedy for curing double-mindedness
Psalm 1:1 – 3	
Psalm 119:9 – 11	
Romans 12:2	
Ephesians 5:25 – 26	
Colossians 3:16 – 17	

7. According to 2 Timothy 3:16–17, what does Scripture accomplish in our lives?

Did You Know?

- Biblical meditation can't be done quickly. The Bible compares it to the process by which roots draw moisture to nurture and bring fruitfulness to a great tree.
- Biblical meditation is so important that it's mentioned more than fifty times in the Old Testament!
- Meditation implies sustained attention and is built around a simple principle: "What the mind repeats, it retains."
- The purpose behind biblical meditation is not to receive a high score on "heaven's entrance exam." Rather, it's for us to become transformed into people from whom goodness flows like an unceasing stream of water.

SMALL GROUP EXPLORATION

God Wants to Guide Us

We need guidance in order to pursue the "one important thing" — God's kingdom and his righteousness — and God provides guidance through the Holy Spirit. If we are to live transformed lives, we must learn to be receptive and responsive to the "leadings" or "promptings" of the Holy Spirit. Let's explore how God chooses to communicate to and guide his people.

1. How do we know God wants to guide us? (See Psalm 25:9; 32:8; Proverbs 3:5 – 6.)

2. What does God say about listening to him? (See John 10:2 – 5, 27.)

3. We aren't always receptive to or discerning of God's guidance. Read the following Scripture passages and note what happened when God had something to say. Then consider what you need to learn about listening for God's voice.

   a. Genesis 28:10 – 22

b. 1 Samuel 3:1–11

c. Numbers 22:10–13, 18–34

4. Psalm 119:97–104 is a psalm of joy and appreciation for God's Word. Note the ways the psalmist has found God's Word to be a source of guidance.

5. God not only speaks to us directly and through his Word, he uses other people to convey his message. Note the different ways God can communicate in each of the following passages.
   a. Acts 4:25

   b. John 12:49–50

   c. Matthew 10:17–20

GROUP DISCUSSION

1. How has what we have explored today influenced your view of what is involved in pursuing God's kingdom?

2. In what specific ways has your appreciation for the importance of biblical meditation changed as a result of this session?

3. Before we explored this session, what did you honestly think was involved in seeking God's guidance? What difference will what we learned today make in how you seek God's guidance in the future?

What Guidance Is ... and Is Not	
Guidance is ...	**Guidance is not ...**
Necessary in order to live life as Jesus would live it if he were in our place. We seek guidance for the growth of our souls, so that we can become the people God has called us to be.	Just a source of "insider" information to help us get what we want — money, happiness, success, etc. Nor is it something we seek only when we're in trouble or facing a difficult decision.
Given by God. Although we seek it, it's not something we earn.	A badge of spirituality or importance.
Active, not passive. Seeking guidance includes praying, exercising judgment and wisdom, taking initiative, and making responsible choices.	A way to avoid taking action. Just being passive and doing whatever comes along does not guarantee we are in God's will.
A process involving choices and risks. God uses guidance to help us become the right kind of people.	A way to avoid taking risks, a shortcut to decision making, or a way for God to get us to perform the right actions.

4. In what new ways have you realized that God could communicate his guidance to us?

PERSONAL JOURNEY: TO DO NOW

1. *God calls us to one thing in life—to pursue his kingdom and his righteousness above all else.* The problem is, we tend to be double-minded: we want to do one thing but do the opposite; we say we're doing one thing while we're really doing something else. The practice of biblical meditation penetrates, cleanses, and transforms our hearts and minds, teaching us how to live fruitful lives for the kingdom of God. As we immerse ourselves in Scripture, we are transformed from double-mindedness to the single focus of pursuing God's kingdom.

   If you asked your family members and/or close friends to describe you in terms of simplicity of heart and double-mindedness, would they say your life is characterized primarily by the desire to seek the kingdom of God and his righteousness? Or would they say you are pursuing many directions?

   Write down the ways *you* would say your life is characterized by double-mindedness or by seeking the kingdom of God above all else.

2. *We need the Holy Spirit's guidance in order to discover how to live as Jesus would live if he were in our place.* The guidance of the Holy Spirit is not reserved for "important," "spiritually mature," or "more spiritual" people; it is available to each of us. The Holy Spirit can and will provide guidance when we seek the kingdom of God above all else. Learning to be receptive and responsive to the leadings or promptings of the Holy Spirit is nonoptional if we are to live transformed lives.

Think about a time when God used the Bible or someone else to give you Spirit-guided wisdom. How did you respond then, and how might you respond differently to God's voice now?

To what extent has God's guidance influenced your life — choices, desires, actions, where you go, who you talk to, where you work?

In what ways might your daily life change if you listened for the Spirit continually, such as pausing during the day to ask God for wisdom?

3. *Seeking God's guidance is an intentional choice. It is not a passive avoidance of responsibility, a shortcut to making decisions, or a way to escape risk.* Seeking God's guidance involves prayer, exercising judgment, wisdom, initiative, choice, and responsibility. To seek God's guidance means learning to listen for the Spirit in all things and to be relentlessly responsive to pursuing God's will. God guides us not so we will perform the right actions but so we will learn how to become the right kind of people, so we will learn how to live in the context of seeking his kingdom.

In what ways have you sought God's guidance as an attempt to gain "insider" information, or to avoid responsibility or risk? What would be a better motivation for seeking his guidance for those situations?

If you were to actively seek God's guidance on a daily basis, how might that strengthen your relationship with him?

PERSONAL JOURNEY: TO DO ON YOUR OWN

There's no better time than right now to begin putting into practice what you've learned today about living an undivided life that is focused on God and his Word. Set aside time within the next few days to do the following:

1. Think about the areas of your life in which you tend to be double-minded and write them down.

2. Prayerfully consider why this is a problem for you and write it down. Are you, for example, fearful, holding on to a secret sin, unwilling to make a particular sacrifice, or focused on things of this world?

3. Then begin digging into what Scripture says about those things. Read not only for information, but meditate on the Scripture and listen for God's wisdom and guidance in those specific areas. If the practice of meditating on Scripture is new for you, the following suggestions will help you get started.

Suggestions for Meditating on Scripture

1. *Ask God to meet you in Scripture.* Acknowledge that he is present with you. Ask him to begin to wash your thoughts. Anticipate that God will speak to you through his Word. You may be deeply moved in reading or be prompted to take a particular course of action.

2. *Read the Bible in a repentant spirit.* Read it with a vulnerable heart, realizing that reading for transformation is different from reading to find information or to prove a point. Resolve to obey the Scriptures.

3. *Meditate on a fairly brief passage or narrative.* Read Scripture slowly. When certain words or thoughts stand out, let them sink into your heart and allow God to use them to speak to you. If you are reading a story, use your imagination to envision the setting and what was happening. "Success" in meditation is not to get through a quantity of Scripture but to get the Scripture through to you.

4. *Take one thought or verse with you through the day.* Fruitful living comes to the person who meditates on Scripture "day and night" (Psalm 1:1–3). Before you go to sleep at night or as soon as you wake up, choose a single piece of Scripture on which to meditate throughout the day. You'll discover wonderful truths!

5. *Allow this thought to become part of your memory.* Memorizing Scripture is a powerful means of transforming your mind. It's not how many words you memorize that matters; it's what happens to your mind as you immerse it in Scripture.

Practicing Servanthood, Finding Freedom

*Humility, if we could ever grow into it,
would not be a burden. It would be an
immense gift. Humility is the freedom
to stop trying to be what we're not, or
pretending to be what we're not, and
accepting our "appropriate smallness."
In Luther's words, humility is the deci-
sion to "let God be God."*

—John Ortberg

QUESTIONS TO THINK ABOUT

1. Define pride and identify the ways it reveals itself in our lives.

2. When you hear the word *servanthood,* what comes to mind? What appeals to you? What repels you?

3. How do you feel when you've pleased someone who is important to you? In what ways does that person's approval influence your thinking and/or future behavior?

VIDEO OBSERVATIONS

The Messiah complex—symptom of pride

The ministries of servanthood

Approval addiction

The discipline of secrecy

VIDEO HIGHLIGHTS

1. In what ways has your view of the practice of servanthood changed or been challenged by what you saw in the video?

2. John Ortberg mentioned several ministries of daily life—the ministry of the mundane, the ministry of interruptions, the ministry of holding your tongue, and so on. How does viewing these daily occurrences as opportunities to practice servanthood change the way we respond to them?

3. Why do you think the discipline of secrecy is hard to practice?

LARGE GROUP EXPLORATION

The Transforming Power of Servanthood

Pride is a persistent human problem. It is so deeply rooted in us that it is even easy to become proud of our spiritual growth! Pride can be so subtle, yet it always leads us to be preoccupied with ourselves and our comparative worth. Whereas Jesus said the essence of spiritual life is to love God and to love people, pride destroys that capacity.

In contrast, the practice of servanthood sets us free from the endless contest to see who is the greatest. It helps us to recognize that the world doesn't revolve around us and in the process trains us in humility. Let's explore the sin of pride and the grace of humility to discover how we can pursue humility in everyday life.

1. How did the serpent tempt Eve to eat the forbidden fruit in the Garden of Eden? (See Genesis 3:4–5.)

2. What are the consequences of pride in our actions and in our hearts? (See Psalm 10:4; Proverbs 11:2; 13:10; 1 Corinthians 13:4.)

3. From the beginning to the end of Scripture, God denounces pride again and again. What is God's response to pride as recorded in the following passages: Leviticus 26:18–19; Proverbs 16:5; Malachi 4:1; and Luke 20:46–47?

4. What symptoms of pride are evident in the parable Jesus told in Luke 18:9–14? (See especially verses 9–12.)

Telltale Signs of Pride

VANITY: Perhaps the most common manifestation of pride, vanity is a preoccupation with our appearance or image.

STUBBORNNESS: This form of pride causes us to shun correction and renders us unable to stop defending ourselves. If someone points out an error or flaw, our response is to evade, deny, or blame.

EXCLUSION: At its deepest level, pride destroys our capacity to love. It leads us to exclude both God and other people from their rightful place in our hearts. We compare ourselves to others and aren't satisfied until we convince ourselves that we are better, smarter, wealthier, etc.

5. In contrast to pride, humility gives us the freedom to stop trying or pretending to be what we're not. It allows us to accept our "appropriate smallness" so we can cease being preoccupied with ourselves and instead focus on and serve other people as Jesus would if he were in our place.

   a. How does the apostle Paul describe the life of humility and servanthood, and who is our example to follow? (See Philippians 2:3–8.)

   b. What did Jesus specifically teach his disciples about servanthood, and who was their example to follow? (See Matthew 20:25–28.)

6. How does God respond to humility? (See Proverbs 3:34; Isaiah 66:2.)

SMALL GROUP EXPLORATION

A Life of Freedom: The Practice of Secrecy

In his book *Celebration of Discipline,* Richard Foster writes, "The grace of humility is worked into our lives through the Discipline of service.... Nothing *disciplines* the inordinate desires of the flesh like service, and nothing *transforms* the desires of the flesh like serving in hiddenness. The flesh whines against service but screams against hidden service. It strains and pulls for honor and recognition."

Foster clearly recognizes how greatly we struggle with pride and bondage to "approval addiction." He also recognizes how important it is for our hearts to be purified and changed by the practices of servanthood and secrecy. As much as we may be inclined to fight against these disciplines, they truly set us free.

1. Cain suffered the earliest recorded case of "approval addiction." How do we know he suffered from this malady of the heart, and what were the consequences? (See Genesis 4:1–8.)

2. The apostle Paul apparently recognized the risks and destructive power of approval addiction. He frequently warned the early church of its dangers.

a. What did Paul reveal about himself in 1 Corinthians 4:3–4?

b. What had Paul learned about approval addiction? (See Galatians 1:10.)

3. Which phrase in John 12:42–43 describes the religious leaders of Jesus' day who refused to commit themselves to becoming Jesus' disciples? From what did these leaders suffer?

4. What is the source of our self-worth? (See Romans 8:38–39; Galatians 3:26–29.)

5. What do 2 Corinthians 5:9–10 and 1 Thessalonians 4:1 reveal about pleasing God?

6. Jesus actually recommended what John Ortberg calls the practice of secrecy, which helps us gain freedom from approval addiction. Read Matthew 6:1–6, 16–18 and note the instruction and examples Jesus used. Also compare the reward he said will come when we follow or reject his instruction.

Matthew 6	Jesus' instruction	Reward for public display of goodness	Reward for practicing secrecy
Verse 1			
Verses 2–4			
Verses 5–6			
Verses 16–18			

GROUP DISCUSSION

1. In *The Life You've Always Wanted,* John Ortberg wrote, "The primary reason Jesus calls us to servanthood is not just because other people need our service. It is because of what happens to us when we serve." We've spent some time exploring pride and humility, approval addiction, and the practices of servanthood and secrecy. What changes inside us that enables us to live as Jesus would live if he were in our place? In contrast, what happens when we don't serve?

2. We read in John 13:14 that Jesus washed the disciples' feet and wanted that to be an example to his disciples. What things today might be similar examples of daily service we can render to others?

3. We often think we're pretty clever about disguising our pride. What are some of the ways we try to impress people without letting on that we're trying to impress them?

4. Jesus was totally free from the need to create an impression and that enabled him to serve his Father completely and to speak God's truth in love without concern for what might happen to him. What do you think would change in your life if you were free from the burden of "impression management," of trying to get other people to think about you in a certain way?

5. What do you think John Ortberg meant when he wrote, "Acts of servanthood done to impress others lose their intrinsic power to help us enter the life of the kingdom"?

PERSONAL JOURNEY: TO DO NOW

1. *Pride is the oldest sin, and no matter what form it takes, it is rooted in our attempt to be like God.* Pride has been a persistent problem for the human race since the Garden of Eden. It leads us to be preoccupied with ourselves and to shun correction. It damages our relationships. At its deepest level, pride causes us to exclude God and other people from their rightful place in our hearts. Whereas Jesus said the essence of spiritual life is to love God and to love people, pride destroys our capacity to love.

   No matter how well hidden they may be, we all have some struggles with pride. Write down at least three areas or instances of pride.

   NOTE: Look especially hard at areas where you are certain you are "right," where relationships are damaged, where you are sensitive to correction (or where people tend to unfairly criticize you!), or where you feel more important than other people.

2. *The practice of servanthood transforms our prideful hearts.* Humility is not about convincing the world that we are something we are not; it is about recognizing the truth that the universe doesn't revolve around us. True servanthood sets us free from the endless contest to see who is the greatest. Jesus calls us to servanthood not just because other people need our service but because of what happens inside us when we serve.

What role does servanthood play in your life?

In what ways has serving other people changed you?

If your life is lacking in service, write down some ways you could begin serving other people and set a date to begin doing them.

3. *True spiritual maturity sets us free from the bondage of approval addiction. It sets us free from the need to congratulate ourselves when we've gotten something right.* Approval addiction means we are motivated to impress others, to seek their applause and approval. It is the opposite of living as Jesus would live in our place. Acts done to impress others are a form of pride and have no value as spiritual training. But by practicing the discipline of secrecy—doing good things for people but not saying anything about it—we can be released from bondage to approval addiction.

   Think about the people by whose judgment you measure your success or failure: parent(s), teachers, neighbors, coworkers, boss, members of your peer group, etc. How much influence do they *really* wield over you?

   Think about the people in your circle of influence. What opportunities do you have to practice doing "secret" things for them? (Give them a gift anonymously? Pray for them? Do a chore for them?)

PERSONAL JOURNEY: TO DO ON YOUR OWN

Take time after this session ends to think about what you discovered today. Set aside some time to do the following, which will help you to apply what you learned.

1. Read "Ways We Can Enter a Life of Servanthood" and write down concrete ways in which you can begin implementing these practices in your daily life.

Ways We Can Enter a Life of Servanthood

Choosing to serve others is an antidote to pride. Following are some practical ways in which you can begin entering a life of service today.

Ministries of servanthood	Practical ideas	My ideas
Choose to be involved in the ministry of the mundane.	Help a colleague at work or help take care of a sick child in the middle of the night so your spouse can sleep. When you serve well, cheerfully, and out of the limelight, you may one day start doing it for the joy of it and begin to understand how life in God's kingdom works.	
Choose to be involved in the ministry of availability.	Be willing to be interrupted, to help other people do what isn't on your schedule. Set aside time so you are available to serve others without an agenda of your own. Ask God for wisdom to know when to be available.	

Choose to be involved in the ministry of holding your tongue.	Instead of demonstrating how much you know or how important you are, choose to say nothing. The fate of the world doesn't rest on you or your accomplishments.	
Choose to be involved in the ministry of bearing one another's burdens.	This may mean praying for someone, offering assistance or a comforting word. It may also mean "bearing with" a difficult person until you learn to love him or her or learn to hear God speak through that person.	

2. Carefully read through "Symptoms of Approval Addiction" and check any symptoms that describe you. Then write down what you intend to do about each problem area.

✓	Symptoms of approval addiction	What I intend to do
	I am often hurt when other people express less than glowing opinions about me.	
	I habitually compare myself to other people.	
	I am competitive in most ordinary situations.	
	I have a nagging sense I'm not important enough or special enough.	
	I envy someone else's success.	

I try to impress important people.	
I'm afraid someone will find out how much I worry about receiving approval.	
My sense of self-esteem depends on whether someone notices how smart, attractive, successful, or _____ I am.	
I find it difficult to love someone who expresses disapproval of me.	
The opinions of others really affect me.	
I measure my accomplishments against those of other people.	
My concern for what others think inevitably leads me to shade the truth.	
I resent the person whose approval I seek because too much of my well-being rests in his or her hands.	
I am consumed by impression management. Much of what I say is to control how other people think of me.	

3. Begin doing "secret" acts of kindness for people in your circle of influence, starting today.

Going the Distance with a Well-Ordered Heart

Above all else, guard your heart, for it is the wellspring of life.

Proverbs 4:23

QUESTIONS TO THINK ABOUT

1. How often have you thought or said, "I need to get my schedule under control"? Why is this so important to us?

    a. What would a more balanced life look like if you had one?

    b. Do you think God wants you to have a balanced life? Why or why not?

2. Identify times of spiritual growth in your life. What were the dominant circumstances in your life during those times? What role (if any) do you think those circumstances played in that growth?

3. What has kept you going when you have had to walk through dark, painful times or times when you didn't know how things would work out?

VIDEO OBSERVATIONS

The illusion of a balanced life

Cultivating a well-ordered heart

The value of suffering with God

Mabel—a person who morphed

Writing our lives together with God

VIDEO HIGHLIGHTS

1. What surprised you about John Ortberg's perspective on a balanced life?

2. How does John Ortberg define a well-ordered heart, and how does it relate to the transformed life we've been exploring in this series?

3. When you hear a story like Mabel's, what speaks to you? What would you like to have in common with her life?

4. How do you feel about writing your story with God? What encourages you? What excites you? What scares you?

LARGE GROUP EXPLORATION

Perseverance Through Suffering

Perseverance is formed by faithful endurance in the midst of hardship. It is the capacity to press on through hardship and finish well. Any truly meaningful human endeavor requires perseverance, and spiritual transformation is no exception. God allows hardship and suffering in the lives of his people to reveal our true values, commitments, and beliefs. Our perseverance through suffering produces character and makes our faith strong, mature, and complete so we can finish the race of life well.

1. The New Testament writers were convinced that faithful endurance amidst hardship was necessary for spiritual maturity. Let's look at a few passages that reveal their perspectives.

   a. What did James write about how suffering benefits us and how to respond to it? (See James 1:2–4.)

   b. What do Hebrews 12:7 and 12:11 teach us about the purpose and work of suffering?

c. According to Hebrews 12:1–3, what does our focus need to be if we are to persevere through suffering? What difference does that focus make?

d. According to Hebrews 11:24–27, Moses is considered one who persevered through trial. How did he do this?

2. Throughout Scripture, Abraham is mentioned as a man of great faith. We see evidence of his courageous and bold faith from the very beginning of his walk with God. But even *his* faith was tested. As he faithfully endured, his faith was refined, strengthened, and perfected. Although his faith was tested a number of times, Abraham's greatest test came when God asked him to sacrifice his son, Isaac—the long-awaited fulfillment of God's promise to him—on Mount Moriah. Let's see what we can learn from his experience. (See Genesis 22:1–12.)

a. How did Abraham respond to God's request (verses 1–3)?

b. How long did it take Abraham to get to the place God had told him to go (verse 4)? What does this reveal about his commitment to obedience? What do you think Abraham might have felt or struggled with during the journey?

c. What evidence do you see that Abraham tenaciously held on to the hope that God would be faithful even though the situation looked hopeless (verses 5–9)?

d. When the moment of truth came, Abraham was willing to do what God had called him to do (verses 10–12). What would have to take place in your heart, in your relationship with God, for you to come to that place?

SMALL GROUP EXPLORATION

The Quest for a Well-Ordered Heart

In Arthurian legend, people devoted themselves to the great quest for the Holy Grail, the ultimate symbol of communion with Christ. Today, the great quest of many people is for a "balanced lifestyle." But in God's kingdom, there is only one goal truly worthy of human devotion: pursuing a well-ordered heart. The transformation of our ordinary, fallen hearts into well-ordered hearts requires a plan of action. We each need to choose a "rule of life," a practice that, when done regularly, will help us know Jesus and grow to be more like him.

1. Instead of telling his followers to have a balanced life, what did Jesus say is the quest worthy of our devotion? (See Matthew 6:33; 10:37–39.)

2. The apostle Paul was known not only for his devotion to Christ, but for his passionate appeals to other believers to pursue Christ. Note what he reveals about following Christ in the following passages.

   a. To what did Paul compare his commitment to Christ in 1 Corinthians 9:25–27? In what way(s) does such a commitment nurture a well-ordered heart?

b. What personal price was Paul willing to pay to accomplish his goal? (See 2 Corinthians 11:24–28.)

3. What does Proverbs 4:23 reveal about the heart—the soul and spirit of our being? (See also Matthew 15:18.)

4. James 3:14–18 contrasts an ordered heart and a disordered heart. Note the source, characteristics, and fruit of each kind of heart.

Kind of heart:	Disordered heart	Ordered heart
Source		
Characteristics		
Fruit		

5. If we are serious about our quest for a well-ordered heart, we need to develop a "rule of life" or plan of action that will help us focus our daily activities toward that goal. The apostle Paul gave us two excellent examples that will help us know Jesus and learn to be more like him.

   a. Write down the "rule of life" found in 1 Corinthians 10:31.

   b. Write down the "rule of life" found in Colossians 3:17.

   c. Now write out your own "rule of life." You may use the Scripture passages above if you would like.

6. What will a well-ordered heart prepare us to do? (See Ephesians 5:1–2.)

GROUP DISCUSSION

1. Why is it so important for us to *intentionally* arrange our lives around the goal of spiritual transformation?

2. John Ortberg says that our problems with "balance" in life have more to do with internal disorder than with external disorder. In what ways do you think this is true?

3. We've explored the idea that a well-ordered heart leads us to love the right thing to the right degree in the right way with the right kind of love. What are some common pitfalls that hinder us from doing this? In which areas do you find this difficult to do?

4. When we think about spiritual transformation, we sometimes think about the "big" things we need to address. But a well-ordered heart takes into account everything, even the "little" things that are part of daily life. Let's look at the list of daily activities highlighted in the box below, and begin listing other things we need to be doing in Jesus' name. Consider how we would do these things differently if we did them in Jesus' name.

Living Life in Jesus' Name

- We could wake up in Jesus' name. When the alarm clock goes off, instead of thinking anxious or regretful thoughts we could rest in the assurance that God controls the day and sustains us!
- We could greet God first thing in the morning and invite him to go through the day with us.
- We could greet people in Jesus' name. We could notice them, look right at them, and listen to them.
- We could drive in Jesus' name — if we dared!
- We could watch television and movies in Jesus' name, not watching so much that it begins to create a disordered heart.
- We could do chores in Jesus' name, offering them as gifts to God.
- We could view our coworkers in Jesus' name — considering them to be valuable people, praying for them, being genuinely interested in their lives and families.
- We could spend money in Jesus' name.

PERSONAL JOURNEY: TO DO NOW

1. *Many of us desire a perfectly balanced, manageable life, but God wants us to pursue a much higher goal.* God wants to craft in each of us a well-ordered heart. A well-ordered heart seeks to follow Jesus and do what he would do. It loves the right thing to the right degree in the right way with the right kind of love. The pursuit of a well-ordered heart is worthy of our devotion, is achievable even in the most desperate situations, and produces good far beyond our sphere of influence.

   How seriously do you want to pursue life in the kingdom of God?

   Is pursuing God's kingdom truly the goal to which you have devoted your life? Why or why not?

   If Jesus were in your place right now, in what way(s) would his actions, words, and thoughts differ from yours?

2. *A well-ordered heart is a transformed heart.* If our ordinary, fallen hearts are to be transformed into hearts that love the right thing to the right degree in the right way with the right kind of love, we need a plan of action. That heart-changing plan of action consists of focusing the events of our daily lives around knowing Jesus and learning how to be more like him. It can be summarized by Paul's admonition in Colossians 3:17 to do everything in the name of Jesus.

Write down your "rule of life" and memorize it.

Write down three daily activities to which you will begin to apply your rule of life.

Then put your rule of life into practice. Keep it in mind as you approach each event or interaction of your day. Focus on Jesus' presence with you, especially during these activities. Ask for his help or guidance in learning to be more like him if he were in your place. Or simply share with him what is on your heart.

3. *A well-ordered heart is perfected by faithful endurance through suffering.* God allows hardship and suffering in our lives to test our faith—to reveal our true values, commitments, and beliefs. God's testing is an act of love in that it refines, strengthens, and perfects our faith. Our perseverance through suffering produces character and makes our faith mature and complete so we can finish the race of life well. When we endure through faith, seeking to know God and to walk through our suffering in partnership with him, we discover a life of freedom, hope, and love—the life we've always wanted!

Think about the hardships and times of testing you have experienced. How do you typically respond to hardship?

In light of what you've learned during this session, how might you approach such times differently in the future? Or as you face a particular trial right now?

What is worth sacrificing or enduring in order to finish the race of life well?

What difference does it make to you that God wants you to walk through life—trials as well as good times—in partnership with him?

The Life You've Always Wanted

Spiritual Disciplines for Ordinary People

John Ortberg, Bestselling Author

You can live a deeper, more spiritual life right where you are.

The heart of Christianity is transformation — a relationship with God that impacts not just our spiritual lives but every aspect of our daily lives. John Ortberg calls readers back to the dynamic heartbeat of Christianity — God's power to bring change and growth — and reveals how and why transformation takes place.

The Life You've Always Wanted offers modern perspectives on the ancient path of the spiritual disciplines. But it is more than just a book about things to do to be a good Christian. It's a road map toward true transformation that starts not with the individual but with the person at the journey's end — Jesus Christ.

As with a marathon runner, the secret to finishing a race lies not in trying harder, but in training consistently — training with the spiritual disciplines. The disciplines are neither taskmasters nor ends in themselves. Rather they are exercises that build strength and endurance for the road of growth. The fruit of the Spirit — joy, peace, kindness, etc. — are the signposts along the way.

Paved with humor and sparkling anecdotes, *The Life You've Always Wanted* is an encouraging and challenging approach to a Christian life that's worth living—a life on the edge that fills an ordinary world with new meaning, hope, change, and joy.

Available in stores and online!

Soul Keeping
Study Guide and DVD

Caring for the Most
Important Part of You

Bestselling Author John Ortberg

In this six-session, video-based small group Bible study, Ortberg shows that caring for your soul is necessary for your Christian life. John shows participants what your soul is, why it is important, how to assess your soul's health, and how to care for it so that we can have a meaningful and beautiful life with God and others. When you nurture your soul, your life in this world will come to make sense again; you can find your way back to God from hopelessness, depression, relationship struggles, and a lack of fulfillment. Your soul's resting place is in God, and John Ortberg wants to take participants to that home.

This study guide with DVD includes a DVD with six video teaching sessions from John Ortberg and a study guide with discussion questions, video notes, and in-between studies.

Sessions include:

1. What Is the Soul?
2. The Struggle of the Soul
3. What the Soul Needs
4. The Practice of Grace
5. The Practice of Gratitude
6. The Practice of Growth

Available in stores and online!

God Is Closer Than You Think

This Can Be the Greatest Moment of Your Life Because This Moment Is the Place Where You Can Meet God

John Ortberg

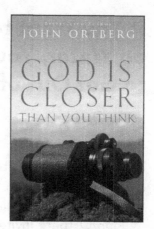

Intimacy with God can happen right now if you want it. A closeness you can feel, a goodness you can taste, a reality you can experience for yourself. That's what the Bible promises, so why settle for less? God is closer than you think, and connecting with him isn't for monks and ascetics. It's for business people, high school students, busy moms, single men, single women ... and most important, it's for YOU.

God Is Closer Than You Think shows how you can enjoy a vibrant, moment-by-moment relationship with your heavenly Father. Bestselling author John Ortberg reveals the face of God waiting to be discovered in the complex mosaic of your life. He shows you God's hand stretching toward you. And, with his gift for storytelling, Ortberg illustrates the ways you can reach toward God and complete the connection — to your joy and his.

Six-Session DVD Study also available.

Available in stores and online!

If You Want to Walk on Water, You've Got to Get Out of the Boat

John Ortberg

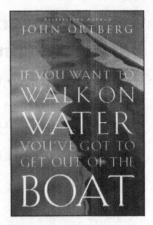

Deep within you lies the same faith and longing that sent Peter walking across the wind-swept Sea of Galilee toward Jesus.

John Ortberg invites you to consider the incredible potential that awaits you outside your comfort zone. Out on the risky waters of faith, Jesus is waiting to meet you in ways that will change you forever, deepening your character and your trust in God. The experience is terrifying. It's thrilling beyond belief. It's everything you'd expect of someone worthy to be called Lord.

The choice is yours to know him as only a water-walker can, aligning yourself with God's purpose for your life in the process. There's just one requirement: *If You Want to Walk on Water, You've Got to Get Out of the Boat.*

Six-Session DVD Study also available.

Available in stores and online!

When the Game Is Over, It All Goes Back in the Box

John Ortberg, Bestselling Author

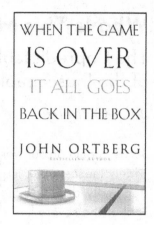

In this thought-provoking look at what's really important in life, John Ortberg uses games as a metaphor to help us recognize and play for life's real prize: being rich toward God.

Told with humor and wisdom by this bestselling author, pastor, and game-strategist, *When the Game Is Over It All Goes Back in the Box* reminds us that everything on earth belongs to God, and everything we "win" is just on loan. Being Master of the Board is not the point; playing by God's rules is. Ortberg makes sure we understand the object of the game, but he also walks us through the set-up, the rules, the strategies, and choosing the right trophies.

This book is for those who want to sort out what's fleeting and what's permanent in God's kingdom. It's the perfect playbook for individuals or groups interested in considering life's true priorities and arranging their lives with eternal prizes in mind.

Six-Session DVD Study also available.

Available in stores and online!

Who Is This Man?

The Unpredictable Impact of the Inescapable Jesus

John Ortberg

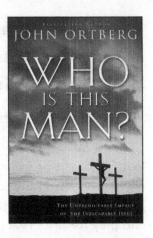

Jesus' impact on our world is highly unlikely, widely inescapable, largely unknown, and decidedly double-edged. It is unlikely in light of the severe limitations of his earthly life; it is inescapable because of the range of impact; it is unknown because history doesn't connect dots; and it is doubled-edged because his followers have wreaked so much havoc, often in his name.

He is history's most familiar figure, yet he is the man no one knows. His impact on the world is immense and non-accidental. From the Dark Ages to post-modernity, he is the Man who won't go away.

And yet ... you can miss him in historical lists for many reasons, maybe the most obvious being the way he lived his life. He did not loudly and demonstrably defend his movement in the spirit of a rising political or military leader. He did not lay out a case that history would judge his brand of belief superior in all future books.

His life and teaching simply drew people to follow him. He made history by starting in a humble place, in a spirit of love and acceptance, and allowing each person space to respond.

His vision of life continues to haunt and challenge humanity. His influence has swept over history bringing inspiration to what has happened in art, science, government, medicine, and education; he has taught humans about dignity, compassion, forgiveness, and hope.

Five-Session DVD Study also available.

Available in stores and online!

The Me I Want to Be

Becoming God's Best Version of You

John Ortberg

In *The Me I Want to Be*, John Ortberg — the bestselling author of *When the Game Is Over, It All Goes Back in the Box*; *God Is Closer Than You Think*; and *The Life You've Always Wanted* — helps you gauge your spiritual health and measure the gap between where you are now and where God intends you to be. Then he provides detailed tasks and exercises to help you live in the flow of the Spirit, circumventing real-world barriers — pain and sorrow, temptations, self-doubt, sin — to flourish even in a dark and broken world.

As you start living in the flow, you will feel:

- a deeper connection with God
- a growing sense of joy
- an honest recognition of your brokenness
- less fear, more trust
- a growing sense of being "rooted in love"
- a deeper sense of purpose

God invites you to join him in crafting an abundant and joy-filled life. *The Me I Want to Be* shows you how to graciously accept his invitation.

Five-Session DVD Study also available.

Available in stores and online!

WILLOW CREEK ASSOCIATION

This resource is just one of many ministry tools published in partnership with the Willow Creek Association. Founded in 1992, WCA was created to serve churches and church leaders striving to create environments where those still outside the family of God are welcomed—and can more easily consider God's loving offer of salvation through faith.

These innovative churches and leaders are connected at the deepest level by their all-out dedication to Christ and His Kingdom. Willing to do whatever it required to build churches that help people move along the path toward Christ-centered devotion; they also share a deep desire to encourage all believers at every step of their faith journey, to continue moving toward a fully transformed, Christ-centered life.

Today, more than 10,000 churches from 80 denominations worldwide are formally connected to WCA and each other through WCA Membership. Many thousands more come to WCA for networking, training, and resources.

For more information about the ministry of the
Willow Creek Association, visit: **willowcreek.com**.